STANDARD LO

Supporting Children in the Early Years

Supporting Children in the Early Years

Edited by
Robin Campbell and Linda Miller

tb
Trentham Books

First published in 1995 by Trentham Books Limited

Trentham Books Limited
Westview House
734 London Road
Oakhill
Stoke-on-Trent
Staffordshire
England ST4 5NP

British Cataloguing in Publication Data
A catalogue record for this book is available from
the British Library.

ISBN: 1 85856 031 4

Designed and typeset by Trentham Print Design
Limited, Chester and printed in Great Britain by
Bemrose Shafron Limited, Chester

Contents

Preface

The purpose of this book is to bring together and disseminate the contributions made during a series of seminars held at the University of Hertfordshire in the Spring and Summer of 1994. During those seminars current research, recent legislation and developments in professional thinking and practice were brought together under the title of 'Supporting Children in the Early Years: From Research to Practice'. The participants represented a range of people working both with and for young children including nursery and primary school teachers, playgroup workers, Under Fives Advisers, Children's Library Service representatives and students engaged in training to be early years teachers. In the last seminar of the series, Margaret Lally expressed her delight and amazement that more than one hundred people should turn out on a hot summer evening, after a busy day in their respective workplaces and in the last week of the school term, to hear her speak. Arguably this collective action expresses the need of those involved in the care and education of young children to be supported in their work through hearing about recent research and developments and to have the opportunity to share these ideas with others working in similar situations.

Prologo

Chapter 1

Support In the Early Years

Linda Miller

The central focus of this book is the support of young children in the earliest stages of learning and development. A number of recent trends, some of which are identified by the *Start Right* report (Ball, 1994), make the topic of supporting young children extremely important at this time. These trends include the lack of specific funding for care and education in the early years, the low employment status of many early years educators, the diversity of pre-school provision, and linked to this, the lack of a supportive framework for parents of young children in a rapidly changing society, also the increased admission of four year olds into primary schools and the lack of trained professionals to work with this age group. Additionally, the downward pressure of the National Curriculum, leading to an over-emphasis upon a 'basic skills' curriculum in the early years (Blenkin and Kelly,1994), is posing a threat to the established principles and practice of early years education, as discussed by Margaret Lally in this text. This is despite the attempts of researchers such as Carol Fox and Robin Campbell to suggest more fruitful and appropriate approaches for fostering learning and development in the early years. Also, as the final chapter notes, the impact of new legislation for identifying and supporting children with special educational needs at the earliest opportunity, poses yet another challenge to early years educators to work in partnership with parents and other professionals, within a supportive framework, so that all children can be provided with an education which meets their needs. As Margaret Lally notes, young children need adults who will support and protect them from the pressure of the trends and changes outlined above, but in order to do this, adults also need sustaining in their work. Most early years educators would contend that despite the rewards, there is nothing more exhausting than spending the day attempting to meet the diverse needs and demands of between 20 and 30 young children. Robin Campbell lists eight key ways in which the adult working with young children might support them; no doubt the list can be added to. Adults, therefore, also need a supportive framework in order that they can bear the weight of the pressures they are facing (Lally, this text).

There are three aspects of support addressed in this text. These are:

- ☐ supporting young children;
- ☐ supporting adults;
- ☐ frameworks for support.

The remainder of this chapter is organised under these headings.

Supporting Young Children

Carol Fox, in her chapter, tells how the five young children in her study, who became accomplished oral story tellers, were supported by their parents by being read stories from a very early age. Just as importantly, they were listened to when telling their stories. Whilst acknowledging that the classroom context of story-telling is different to that of the home, she emphasises the value of teachers continuing this support by reading many stories a day, some taped or on records, some read by visiting parents. The needs of children who have not had this opportunity at home are particularly stressed.

I like Carol Fox's notion of the home environment providing a safe ground within which children can experiment with even their rudest stories. The parents in her study did not reject anything that was offered in a story, thus assisting their children's riskiest ventures. Learning for both children and adults is about taking risks (Harste et.al. 1994). Fox suggests teachers can also take risks by moving away from repetitive practice such as 'News' time, and providing supportive opportunities for children to tell longer stories not related to real life events, including the chance to act out their stories in play situations.

The theme of the adult as a key support in children's literacy development is continued by Robin Campbell. He emphasises six literacy activities within which adults in the nursery classroom can offer an important supporting role. He then goes on to describe eight ways in which this support might be offered.

In order to assist children in their learning and development, Margaret Lally stresses the role of the adult in creating favourable conditions for learning. She argues that early years educators must buttress children from a curriculum and related practices which militate against independence, making choices and taking responsibility for their own learning. She highlights the need for early years workers to be able to see children's learning and development with a trained and professional eye (Drummond, 1993); an eye which is not clouded by a vision of a National Curriculum Key Stage 1 child.

Two very individual examples of supporting children with special educational needs are given by Sheila Wolfendale and Janine Wooster. They describe how Mohammed and Fowsia and their families receive a network of support from adults representing a range of disciplines, in order to provide them with an inclusive education which meets their needs.

Supporting Adults

The need for adults to communicate and to support each other, with the common aim of furthering children's learning and development, is highlighted throughout this text. In the case of parents and teachers, it is important that each knows the contribution which the other is making to the child's development. It seems sad that, as in Carol Fox's study, at least one teacher was totally unaware of two children's considerable oral storying skills, believing the children to have a language problem because they didn't talk much in school (Fox,1994). Also, that teachers' expectations of the ways in which parents support their young children, in this instance in helping with reading, was either not known about or doubted by teachers (see also Hannon and James,1990). Inviting parents into the classroom to continue with this help, provides both teachers and children with much needed assistance.

Such links between home and school may enable children to make a smooth transition into what is a 'new world' (Gregory and Biarnes, 1994). As Margaret Lally's chapter shows, our assessments of young children can be greatly enriched by finding out about the knowledge and skills which have been demonstrated in the home setting. Sharing this knowledge with parents can have a two way effect. Parents will feel that their knowledge about their child is valued, but also, early years educators will have the opportunity to articulate what they are trying to achieve, to explain what they are doing and why (Gregory and Biarnes, 1994); thus increasing the likelihood of parental support. Lally offers an example of how some work on pulleys in a nursery was further enriched for one child through a home related experience. If early years educators talk and work together with parents in this way, parents cannot be made an excuse for bad practice, similar to those offered as examples by Lally, e.g. 'We do it this way because the parents expect it....'. Lally also stresses the need for early years staff to work in partnership and support each other, particularly in sharing information about children as they move into new settings.

The need for back-up from colleagues, in the face of new legislation resulting in changed practices, is highlighted vividly by Wolfendale and Wooster. Many of the people requiring support when threatened by change, were themselves working within a support capacity with children with special educational needs and their families. Their chapter describes the development of a comprehensive and multi-disciplinary framework of support for young children with special educational needs in the London borough of Newham.

Frameworks for Support

I have followed Margaret Lally's example in offering a dictionary definition of some key words. Support is already defined by Margaret in her chapter. A framework is defined as: 'an essential supporting structure' (Allen, 1991). Frameworks for support are not always obvious or explicit. Carol Fox writes about the way in which the experience of hearing stories told or read aloud can offer a framework within which young learners can be encouraged and sustained in their early attempts at writing and oral story telling. She suggests how further support can be offered through sensitive classroom planning i.e. circle time, in which children can share fantasy stories and the provision of audio cassettes to facilitate the telling of stories and listening to recorded stories.

Robin Campbell offers a more explicit framework as he analyses what it is the adult does in supporting the child's literacy development. He describes how a model of reading is demonstrated for the child as the adult reads both with and for children. In sharing books and stories with children we see that the early years educator skilfully recognises when to interject, comment, question and reinforce the child's offerings. Campbell also shows how learning about literacy can be presented in a way which subscribes to the principles of early years education that are discussed by Lally. He describes how learning about books and stories is brought to life by the teacher in a nursery class as she engages the children in helping to cook and eat the three bears' porridge. Thus, he highlights the importance of a well planned literacy environment in which children can move forward in their learning and development.

The need for early years workers to be clear about the principles which underpin their professional practice is emphasised by Margaret Lally. She argues that these are the foundations upon which good early years practice is built. The importance of principles which are derived from both the evidence of research and reflections upon practice (hence the title of the seminar series) are stressed. Lally believes that without a clear rationale on which to base their work with young children, early years workers will be vulnerable to pressures which damage early years practice: in such cases they would be unable to protect and support the children with whom they work. She describes how groups of early years workers have been empowered by strong principles, which can help to develop practice which supports children in ways they know to be right.

In Chapter 5 more conspicuous frameworks for support are described by Wolfendale and Wooster, particularly for young children with special educational needs.. They report how the 1993 Education Act and Code of Practice has tightened up the framework in which the needs of children are identified, assessed and responded to. Forms of support arising from legislative frameworks are outlined, for example parental involvement projects in the pre-school years, such as Portage, and parental involvement in assessment from the earliest years.

Other key developments are included relating to children's rights and equal opportunities, although as Wolfendale notes, progress on the former leaves much room for improvement. Having a Minister for Health who appears openly to condone smacking young children does nothing to further this cause. Wolfendale and Wooster suggest that moves towards anti-racist and equal opportunities policies in early years care and education, have been more visible with written policy documents providing a framework for good practice. The need for an inclusive education system which will embrace and uphold the needs and rights of all children and their parents, is discussed as a major component of equal opportunities and rights issues. How these principles can operate in practice is described by Janine Wooster in relation to her work in Newham. However, the equal opportunities issue of a cohesive framework of pre-school provision to support young children and their families, the lack of which is highlighted as a threat to young children's welfare at the beginning of this chapter, remains largely unfulfilled.

Summary

A number of ways forward for supporting children in the early years are outlined in this introductory chapter and are expanded upon in subsequent chapters. What is clear, is that the nature of support is interactive. Children need supportive parents and informed early years educators to assist them in their learning and development. In turn, adults working with young children need support. They need support from each other and they need the support that comes from external frameworks. The seminar series which gave rise to this book, has contributed in part to that framework.

References

Allen, E. (1991) (Ed.) *The Concise Oxford Dictionary of Current English: Eighth Edition.* London: BCA.

Ball, C. (1994) *Start Right.* London: RSA.

Blenkin, G. and Kelly, V. (Eds.) (1994) *The National Curriculum and and Early Learning: an Evaluation.* London: Paul Chapman.

Drummond, M.J. (1993) *Assessing Children's Learning.* London: David Fulton.

Gregory, G. and Biarnes, J. Tony and Jean Francois. (1994) Looking for sense in the strangeness of school. In Dombey, H. and Meek-Spencer, M. (Eds.) *First Steps Together.* Stoke-on-Trent: Trentham Books/IEDPE.

Hannon, P. and James, S. (1990) Parents' and teachers' perspectives on pre-school literacy development. *British Educational Research Journal.* 16, 3. pp 259-272.

Harste, J.C., Woodward, V.A., Burke, C.L. (1984) *Language Stories and Literacy Lessons.* New Hampshire: Heinemann Educational Books.

Chapter 2

Principles to practice in early years education

Margaret Lally

Support: *'to bear the weight of', 'to help with sympathy or practical advice', 'to approve of and encourage', 'to be in favour of', 'to be loyal to'* (Longman, 1978)

Young children are vulnerable. Loyalty, approval, help, encouragement and sympathy are exactly what they need from adults. They also need adults who are prepared to bear the pressure which all early years workers are facing, which threatens to dominate children's experience.

There is growing evidence that adults are not protecting children from the pressure (Blenkin and Kelly,1994). Two recent experiences reminded me powerfully of what we and children have lost, or are in danger of losing. On a visit to Holland I saw role play and interactive storytelling of a quality I rarely see in the UK these days. Then I met an early years specialist from another part of the world who expressed the view that the National Curriculum was having a negative effect on education in the UK. She described how she and her colleagues used to visit to be inspired by our nursery and infant practice. She felt there was still some exciting practice, but that they now also look elsewhere in Europe.

These experiences are sobering, but also useful, because they help us to focus more clearly on what from our past traditions we need to protect. But how will those newer to early years work gain access to our heritage? Teacher trainers say they are no longer allowed to teach child development and that the emphasis on National Curriculum subject study has undermined specialist early years courses. This has serious implications for the future of the profession and for children's experience in school.

If we are to continue to support children it is vital that all early years workers are clear about the principles which should underpin their work. Bruce (1987) set out 10 common principles drawn from the work of the pioneers in early childhood education. These principles were developed further by the Early Years Curriculum Group (EYCG, 1989, 1992). Many early years practitioners have looked at these principles and most would claim to agree with them. However, during in-service training sessions, when workers start to consider what each of these principles means and how it influences their practice, it quickly becomes apparent that the same words mean different things to different people, and that there is often no clear view of how each principle might translate into practice. Although workers say they believe the principles, there is often a mismatch between what they say they believe and what they actually do with the children. This mismatch is interesting since, if we really believe something, our actions reflect this belief. It highlights the need for early years workers to define their own set of principles.

What are principles and where do they come from?

Principle: *'a general truth or belief that is used as a base for reasoning or action, or for the development of further ideas'* (Longman, 1978).

Principles are concerned with what we believe, and must underpin everything we do. This seems obvious, and yet many early years workers find it difficult to talk about what they believe. If asked to write down their principles (e.g. in relation to parental involvement) they frequently write down what they do, rather than what they believe. This is, perhaps, because they are more used to talking about their practice. However, unless we have a rationale for this practice, we find we are unable to explain it to others.

Early years workers need to recognise that their own personal beliefs are not enough, and that principles must be derived from, and supported by, evidence drawn from the research and theory of early childhood education and child development. Evidence to support principles also comes from workers' experience with, and observations of, children. The evidence we ourselves collect helps us to make sense of what others write, and of the principles offered to us by others. When we see in children in our groups characteristics and behaviour which researchers have spent years studying, it is very exciting. In this way, observation enables us to make our own the principles offered by experts in the field.

Why are principles important? How can they support us?

Principles are important because they provide a foundation for our thinking and our practice. If we work from a clearly defined and understood set of principles, we are enabled to be confident about what we do. Mary Jane Drummond (1993) writes: 'Good pre-school and primary practice must be built on a solid foundation of both conviction and rationale' (p.111). Early years practitioners are often strong on conviction — in other words they can say very firmly what they think is, or is not, good practice — but are often weaker when asked to say why.

Early years workers find 'why' questions difficult and sometimes get defensive if asked to give reasons for their practice. They need to understand that, if they cannot give confident answers to questions, they are weak on rationale and their practice is therefore vulnerable to pressure from outsiders. Early years teachers who say things like 'I know it's not right but the head expects me to do this' or 'the parents want to see work in books' or 'we've got to do this because of the National Curriculum' are not using principles to help them rationalise their work. They are using others as a justification or excuse for their practice. They have not been able to use their principles to explain a developmentally appropriate approach and are therefore influenced by everything except the children in their groups. These practitioners are not able to support young children because they do not have a solid base of principles to support the development of their practice in the context of a changing educational scene.

Other practitioners, by using their clearly defined principles, have been able to resist the same kinds of pressure. A group of nursery and reception teachers who had attended a course together in the London Borough of Tower Hamlets used their firm principles as a starting point for developing and publishing an approach to planning the early years curriculum (THEIABU, 1993). This has enabled them to resist the top-down pressure to plan in ways which they considered inappropriate, and to devise a rigorous approach which has been well accepted by colleagues.

A second example concerns a multi-disciplinary group of practitioners working with under fives in the Royal Borough of Kensington and Chelsea. This group worked from their principles to develop and publish an approach to assessment which offers a more positive, ongoing approach to recording children's achievements than baseline tests. Their Early Years Profile for 3-5 year olds (RBKC, 1992) has been adapted by those working with children under the age of three, and some schools in the borough are now continuing the Profile throughout Key Stage 1 and 2.

A third example concerns an individual reception class teacher who, whilst attending a course on observation skills, was able to use her observations of children in her group to help, first herself, and then others in her school, understand why four year olds need access to their own outdoor area. She made a case for expenditure, and a fenced-off area has been provided.

These examples demonstrate how empowering strong principles can be. They enable workers to take responsibility for their own practice and to gain respect from their colleagues and others. Most importantly, they enable workers to resist settling for second-best for children and guide them towards alternative approaches when under pressure.

Which principles need to underpin early years practice?

If adults are to support young children's development and learning, it is particularly important that the following four principles are understood and translated into practice. These principles remind us of what it really means to be an educator of young children — rather than someone who merely delivers a curriculum.

1. **'There is potential in all children which emerges powerfully under favourable conditions'**
   (EYCG, 1989 p.3)

This is primarily a principle of equality. The current educational climate with its emphasis on curriculum content and delivery is leading some early years staff to forget that it is their responsibility to create favourable conditions for learning. It is depressing to hear teachers saying things like 'well, they're reception (or year 1 or year 2) now so they've got to ...'

What is getting lost here is the notion of education as a seamless robe (ESAC, 1988), and the understanding that there is no such thing as a typical 4 year old or a 6 year old, let alone a reception child or a year 1 child.

It used to be recognised that young children are individuals, at different stages of development, with different life experiences and with different learning approaches — e.g. some like to stand and observe, some prefer a more direct hands-on approach, some like to move quickly from one activity to another — not necessarily flitting but often making connections in their thinking and their actions (Athey, 1990). In short, it used to be understood that children needed an approach which respected their individuality. Children's needs have not changed, but perhaps the emphasis on content delivery is damaging adult perceptions.

Children are increasingly being seen in terms of what they cannot do, or what they should be able to do at a particular age. This view is behind some approaches to baseline assessment where children are being tested on attainment targets as soon as they start school. The effect of these tests is to write some children off after a few days. After all, what kind of a view does a teacher gain of a child who receives very few ticks on the test sheet?

Research evidence shows us clearly that we should be much more cautious about our assessments of young children. Children engage in richer talk at home than at school (Tizard and Hughes, 1984, Wells, 1986) and the context in which assessment takes place makes a difference to what we find out about children (Donaldson 1978, Hughes, 1986). Often expectations of children are too low (Tizard et. al. 1988), and workers need to accept that their view of a child is sometimes inaccurate and always incomplete. Above all, workers need to make more effort to fit the learning context to the child rather than expecting every child to fit their expectations.

In order to translate this principle into practice early years workers need to recognise that:

Transitions need sensitive management — All moves from one setting to another are potentially stressful and no-one (including adults!) can demonstrate their competence when they are still settling into a new situation. Early years workers need to acknowledge this and ensure that they create an environment where all children can develop high self-esteem and confidence. All children need to feel they belong, and that they are valued members of the group. There is a real danger that, in the pursuit of the academic curriculum, these important emotional and social influences on learning will be devalued. When transitions are not managed well for individual children they react in two main ways. Some children withdraw and eventually become the 'quiet ones' — they often become invisible! Others rebel and demand attention. Rather than labelling these children, workers should analyse the messages they are giving and consider how individual needs could be met.

Children need to be offered independence, choice and responsibility — In order to create favourable conditions for all children there needs to be some flexibility in early years provision. Children need opportunities to become independent, make choices and take responsibility because in these ways they can show their individuality — they can show what they are thinking and what they can do in a very positive way (David, Curtis and Siraj-Blatchford, 1992). If children are tightly controlled in a group setting they have no opportunity to show their real potential. In classes where all their time is directed by adults, children stop asking questions, being curious and enthusiastic and their potential can get lost. However, in classes which offer independence, choice and responsibility, children learn to feel capable and competent and their achievements often exceed adult expectations.

Experiences and resources should have direct relevance to, and should motivate the children — All children need to see their own personal experiences reflected back to them if they are to feel they belong and can relax in a group setting. The learning context is therefore very important and early years teams need to try to see it through the eyes of particular children and families and adapt it accordingly. For example, a group of teachers supporting traveller families made some beautiful caravans for the schools the children attended. These caravans are small versions of the real thing and enable the children to feel 'I belong here. This place welcomes me. There is something relevant to my life here'. All children need to feel these things and early years workers need to monitor their provision to ensure it is both relevant and motivating.

Adults need to take a personal interest in each child — Adults need to observe and listen to children and give them personal time. This seems very obvious, but as children move through school it is all too easy for them to be regarded as a group, rather than as individuals in their own right — it is this aspect of the reception class which many four year olds find most difficult. All children need to feel that adults notice them sometimes and pay attention to the things they do well. It is particularly important that children who have difficulty settling into school can feel that their strengths are being noticed and that they receive positive encouragement and feedback. Observations can help workers understand the support each child needs. For example a refugee child, newly arrived from a war zone, was observed in his infant class leaving the work-sheet he had been given and going into the home corner where he started to pull the arms and legs off a doll. The nursery nurse was asked to bring him back to his work. Clearly the work-sheet did not motivate him — probably because it made no sense to him. However, his actions in the home corner could lead us to reflect on the life experiences which might now be driving him. Rather than expecting the nursery nurse in the class to keep him at the work-sheet, it would be more productive to encourage her to give him some personal time to enable him to cope with being in the alien environment of school. This child, like many others, has a specific set of individual needs which demand the adult's personal attention. His needs also demand the kind of flexible learning environment referred to above.

Early years staff need to work in partnership with each other and with each child's parents — If workers are to begin to understand children's potential, and to raise their expectations of the individuals in their groups, they must talk with the other adults in the children's lives. It can be frustrating to be told by a colleague that a child we knew to be competent in all kind of ways, has suddenly, after transfer, become someone who cannot do anything! Perceptions of a child can be very different even within the same nursery team, but there is often a real mismatch between the expectations of the adults in the setting a child is leaving and the new adults in her life. This is because the adults the child is leaving knew that child at her most confident and competent. In the new setting the child still has to gain confidence and show what she can do. This is why it is so important that early years staff listen to, and take notice of, what the child's parents and staff in any previous setting have to say. A regular, ongoing dialogue with parents is also important to provide information about the child's learning. A child in a nursery school had been involved in some work on pulleys to link with building work going on nearby. A couple of weeks later his mother told his teacher that at the weekend they had gone past the building site and he wanted to stop. He was able to explain to her exactly how the pulley worked and she was so impressed she wanted to tell the teacher. Without this conversation, the teacher would not have known how much he had taken in from the experiences she had offered. He was a child who said very little at school but at home he talked a lot about his school learning. If there is no dialogue between staff and parents there is a risk that a child's abilities and potential will be seriously underestimated.

2. **'Learning is most effective when children are actively involved and not passive recipients of information'** (David, Curtis, Siraj-Blatchford, 1992 p.12)

This principle is concerned with how children learn or the learning process and it has been under threat from those who think that learning is a direct result of teaching. Holt (1991) sums up what he learnt as a teacher

> The seven word version is 'learning is not the product of teaching'. The five word version is 'teaching does not make learning'. As I mentioned before, organised education operates on the assumption that children learn only when and only what and only because we teach them. This is not true. It is very close to one hundred percent false. Learners make learning, learners create learning. (p.160)

Anyone who has worked with young children knows the truth in this and also that children need to be actively involved in their learning. So why is it that some adults are trying to make children become passive recipients? Why do some early years staff in both nursery and infant settings think it is acceptable to give children endless seat-based activities including work-sheets and handwriting drills?

By adding a further principle we can see more clearly what young children need:

'An appropriate curriculum first strengthens children's behavioural knowledge and then introduces them to abstract representations directly related to it'
(Katz and Chard, 1989 p.23)
Children extract knowledge and understanding from the experiences they are having. A reception teacher had set up an interactive display which enabled children to explore pouring a range of substances into containers of different shapes and sizes. One child spent a lot of time at this display pouring back and forth. In fact he wanted to spend so much time that the teacher admitted she got a bit nervous — should she be moving him on, should she put the display away? etc. But then she had an interesting experience. She had filled the sand tray with wooden beads and provided a range of containers. She wanted the children to estimate how many beads each container would hold and which container would hold the most. What she discovered was that the boy described above was the only child who could make a sensible estimate. All the pouring had enabled this child to cope with the abstract thinking involved with the task and this example supports Katz and Chard's point that 'the developmental sequence seems to be from behavioural to representational knowledge, although the two forms of knowledge increasingly interact with each other as the child grows.' (p.23)

Adults need to support young children's learning by enabling them to engage in the behaviours which will give them access to different kinds of knowledge and understanding. Young children need opportunities to behave like mathematicians, scientists, readers and writers etc. because through behaving in these ways they actually generate knowledge and understanding for themselves. They make their own learning.

Some further evidence of what children need from adults if their learning is to be supported comes from the work of Elliot and Dweck (1988) and Dweck and Leggett (1988). Their work indicates that children who are required by adults to carry out tasks with performance goals can become helpless and stop putting in effort because they fear failure or have experienced failure in the past. These children stop being learning oriented. This research challenges early years workers to consider how they can develop a curriculum for 'mastery' rather than a performance oriented curriculum — how they can offer children the chance to master things for themselves and tackle difficult problems without fear, rather than perform for an adult. (Sylva, 1994)

Since some elements of a curriculum for performance can be seen in nursery and infant settings, there is work to be done on translating this principle into practice. First, early years workers need to ask some hard questions about the work-sheet and other similar adult directed activities. Are the activities on offer about learning or about time-filling? Are we merely occupying children or are they really challenged both mentally and physically?

Second, children need a to be offered a range of opportunities to engage in behaviours relevant to all areas of learning and experience (DES, 1989). These opportunities arise when children come into contact, through first-hand experience, with materials and with more experienced children or adults. They also arise when high quality play provision and contexts are set up to enable children to represent and extend their learning. Role play is particularly important in both nursery and infant settings and yet its potential as a rich context for the development of behavioural understanding has not always been exploited.

In one nursery school the children had visited the local railway station to gather first-hand experience. This visit was followed up with a great deal of talk with staff acting as scribes as the children represented and recorded their visit orally. This recorded talk was on display for visitors to look at and talk about with the children. Talk provides young children with their most efficient method of representing and recording their experiences. The children had also been enabled to represent their experience through role-play in and out of doors and also through model making which inspired further role-play — some of the children had made a paper railway track which went right round the nursery along which they could drive their trains.

This kind of first-hand experience and play can be extended throughout the infant and junior school (Hall and Abbott 1991). However, plans need to be made for ensuring progression. In some schools staff are working together to plan for progression in play provision. They have recognised that the quality of play often deteriorates as children move from the nursery, and are taking steps to ensure that it can still provide a rich learning context.

Finally, in order to monitor whether children are enabled to be actively involved in their learning, there needs to be a clear view of what an active learner looks like. The following headings or criteria have been drawn from work with early years staff and parents who all agree that these are the processes children need to be involved in if they are to learn.

Active learning involves:

— sensory exploration

— exploring ways of using the body

— experimenting with ways of using materials and tools

— practising and refining skills

— setting and tackling problems

— observing and imitating others

— concentration, involvement, being absorbed

— making connections between one experience and another

— talking about experiences/discoveries — collaborating

— asking questions

This list includes mental as well as physical processes and can be used by early years staff to monitor the experience of the children they work with. The last item on the list, asking questions, is particularly interesting. When early years staff are asked to note down questions they hear young children asking both in home and community and school contexts, they nearly always find that school questions are not as varied or deep as questions children ask in their home and in their community. This is partly because there is not the same degree of intimacy in group settings, but it also seems to be because schools do not offer the kind of environment where children are encouraged to question. This is a pity, since children's questions can tell us a lot about them as individuals and as learners, and about their feelings, their ideas, and their interests. All early years workers need to ask: 'Are we creating an environment where children can flourish as active learners?'

3. **'The curriculum for under fives should be broad and balanced with a strong emphasis on children's social, linguistic and physical development'** (OFSTED 1994 p.56)
This principle is concerned with curriculum content for under fives in nursery and reception classes. It is crucial that social, linguistic and physical development have a central role in this curriculum. Positive relationships, effective communication skills and well-developed fine and gross motor skills provide an essential foundation for learning. This principle reminds us that children need a broad, balanced curriculum and that the '3Rs' should not be allowed to dominate at the expense of other equally important areas of learning.

There are some important implications for practice. Early years workers must ensure the young child's need for breadth and balance is recognised in any curriculum plans. They must resist the pressure to concentrate on the media-defined 'basics' (i.e. the 3Rs) and inform the general public of the real basics (personal and social education). They must also resist the temptation to fragment children's learning and must develop the skills of observation which will enable them to demonstrate how a child can be learning across several subject disciplines when engaged in one activity or experience. (EYCG,1992). They must distinguish between coverage and learning. Marching children round the provision to ensure they have covered what is offered is not achieving curriculum breadth — it is merely giving children tasters. Observations can help to show how children can experience a broad curriculum when they work in depth in one area of provision such as water or blocks. Fragmenting children's time is as counter-productive to learning as fragmenting their experiences, and early years teams need to consider whether their daily routine is in the children's best interests — in particular whether it offers long periods of uninterrupted time.

4. Early years education is a specialism requiring specialist initial and in-service training.

This principle has been recognised in recent years largely because early years education as a specialism is seen to be under threat. There is a shortage of nursery-trained teachers and many working with under fives are not appropriately trained. Early years training courses have also been damaged, as mentioned earlier.

Local Management of Schools (LMS) has led to teachers and nursery nurses being replaced by cheaper, less well-qualified staff in some areas, in spite of the fact that recent reports have highlighted the need for well-trained nursery and reception staff (ESAC, 1989, DES, 1990, OFSTED 1993). Without specialist training, workers are rarely able to support children's development and learning effectively (Lally, 1991).

The implications of this principle are clear. Parents, governors and headteachers must insist on the best possible staff to work with younger children. If teachers are not nursery-trained they should be given opportunities to retrain. Teachers also have a responsibility to know their own limitations and should ask for training opportunities, read early childhood texts and visit other establishments. They need to understand that it is not acceptable to learn on the job and get experience at the expense of a group of children. All children deserve better.

All early years workers need to be prepared to go on learning about their specialism by observing, analysing and reflecting upon what happens in their classes. They must use this information to ask for the tools they need to support the children's development and learning. It is at least partly the responsibility of early years staff that so many four year olds have found themselves in such unsuitable provision — children need adults who will not settle for inappropriate staffing ratios, space and equipment. They also need nursery and infant staff to plan together in the interests of continuity and progression.

Early years workers must take responsibility for raising awareness of early years as a specialist area of work. The Government's proposals for a one-year early years teacher training course have been defeated but there is more to be done.

From principles to excitement

Behind all of the principles explored in this chapter is the firm belief that our approach to supporting young children must be guided by the children themselves. The great pleasure in early years work is to learn about the children and to put that learning into practice. A Dutch teacher had been inspired by Gussin Paley (1990) to learn from observing the children in her class in story-telling contexts. She reflected on her observations and developed her practice to take account of the children's enthusiasms. The teacher said that she was so excited that she could not wait to come to school each morning. How many English teachers feel like that! Principles, based on children's needs, can guide us towards practice which inspires and enthuses everyone involved. Young children deserve and need adults who are prepared to work from principles to develop their work in ways which retain the excitement in learning.

References:

Athey, C. (1990) *Extending Thought in Young Children: A Parent Teacher Partnership.* Paul Chapman: London.

Blenkin, G. and Kelly, V. (Eds) (1994) *The National Curriculum and Early Learning: An Evaluation.* Paul Chapman: London.

Bruce, T. (1987) *Early Childhood Education.* Hodder and Stoughton: Sevenoaks.

David, T., Curtis, A. and Siraj-Blatchford, I. (1992) *Effective Teaching in the Early Years: Fostering Children's learning in Nurseries and in Infant Classes.* Trentham Books: Stoke- on Trent.

DES (1989) *Aspects of Primary Education.* The Education of Children Under Five. HMSO: London.

DES (1990) *Starting with Quality.* HMSO: London.

Donaldson, M. (1978) *Children's Minds.* Fontana: Glasgow.

Drummond, M.J. (1993) *Assessing Children's Learning.* David Fulton: London.

Dweck, C.S. and Leggett, E. (1988) A Social- Cognitive Approach to Motivation and Personality. *Psychological Review,* 95 (2) 256-273.

Elliot, E. and Dweck, C.S. (1988) Goals: An Approach to Motivation and Achievement. *Journal of Personality and Social Psychology,* 54 (1) 5-12.

ESAC (1988) *Educational Provision for the Under Fives.* HMSO: London.

EYCG (1989) *Early Childhood Education, the Early Years Curriculum and the National Curriculum.* Trentham Books: Stoke-on-Trent.

EYCG (1992) *First Things First. Educating Young Children.* Madeleine Lindley: Oldham.

Gussin-Paley, V. (1990) *The Boy Who Would be a Helicopter.* Harvard, USA.

Hall, N. and Abbott, L. (1991) *Play in the Primary Curriculum.* Hodder and Stoughton: Sevenoaks.

Holt, J. (1991) *Learning All the Time.* Education Now: Ticknell, Derbyshire.

Hughes, M. (1986) *Children and Number.* Blackwell: Oxford.

Katz, L. and Chard, S. (1989) *Engaging Children's Minds. The Project Approach.* Ablex Publishing Corporation: Norwood, New Jersey.

Lally, M. (1991) *The Nursery Teacher in Action.* Paul Chapman: London

Longman (1978) *Dictionary of Contemporary English.* Longman Group: Essex.

OFSTED (1993) *First Class. The Standards and Quality of Education in Reception Classes.* HMSO: London.

OFSTED (1994) *Handbook for the Inspection of Schools*. HMSO: London.

RBKC (1992) *Early Years Profile and Under Threes Profile.* Isaac Newton Professional Development Centre: Royal Borough of Kensington and Chelsea, London.

Sylva, K. (1994) The Impact of Early Learning on Children's Later Development in Ball, C. (1994) *Start Right. The Importance of Early Learning. Appendix C.* RSA: London.

THEIABU (1993) *Planning in the Early Years.* Tower Hamlets Learning Design Centre: London.

Tizard, B. and Hughes, M. (1984) *Young Children Learning.* Fontana: London.

Tizard, B., Blatchford, P., Burke, J., Farquhar, C. and Plewis, I. (1988) *Young Children at School in the Inner City.* Lawrence Erbaulm Associates: Hove.

Wells, G. (1986) *The Meaning Makers. Children Using Language and Using Language to Learn.* Hodder and Stoughton: Sevenoaks.

Chapter 3

Storytelling at Home and at School

Carol Fox

In my book *At the Very Edge of the Forest* (1993) I have given a very full account of the many detailed analyses I made on the invented oral stories of five young children, age three and a half to five. Here I should like to outline some of the main findings and draw from them some implications for the literacy education of pre-school and infant children in the 1990s. Some of these implications are based on informal conversations I have participated in recently, with parents of reception, Year 1 and Year 2 children at a Brighton Primary school. Others come from my work at the University of the Witwatersrand in Johannesburg in South Africa, in the Summer months of 1994. These insights post-date the reflections about education with which I concluded my book.

The children who invented stories and told them into the tape recorder in my study, had not started full-time school, or were just beginning it. They were white, and, in terms of their parents' education and more particularly their parents' knowledge of children's books, middle-class. They approximate in British terms to the group Shirley Brice Heath calls 'Maintown' in *Ways With Words* (1983). In other ways the children's backgrounds have individual circumstances which do not fit comfortably with a stereotypical notion of 'privilege', a notion often included in the term; middle-class' in educational contexts. Four of the children had separated parents, though all got on well with both parents. All had been read stories from a very early age, and had been told improvised stories too. Four of the five had attended playgroups/nursery schools, so that by the time they entered school at five they would have experienced thousands of story-readings and tellings, both at home and outside home. I undertook my study of these children's invented oral stories to show that the impact of hearing so many stories before school started was enormous, and affected their linguistic, narrative, and cognitive development profoundly. Teachers who claim that their pupils have heard very few or no stories before school might reflect on what one story a day (just before hometime) means in terms of a child's total story experience. One story a day for the whole class cannot begin to compete with the rich story background many children bring with them from home. Many stories a day, especially for those children who have not heard stories at home, would perhaps begin to compensate. The children in my study did plenty of other things beside listening to stories — they played with toys and games, ran about outside, painted and drew etc. Children's picture story books do not necessarily take a long time to read aloud, and it is possible to fit a lot of brief story sessions into a day as well as more intensive ones. This would certainly be necessary if children are to hear their favourite stories repeated, repeated sufficiently often to internalise them, know the words, and have time to absorb their meanings over a long period. The two five year olds in my study, Josh and Sundari, spent some time listening to favourite stories on tapes and gramophone records, and on the radio. Children these days are quite capable of coping with this equipment by themselves, and taped stories are an ideal way to give them the repetitions of stories that they need. Though there are many excellent commercial tapes available, teachers can also make their own using the books in the classroom.

The stories in my study were collected by parents in entirely natural, everyday circumstances at home. The parents did not coerce the children into telling stories if they did not want to, did not suggest what the story material might be, did not rule out genres which adults might regard as non-story (poems, songs, news broadcasts and weather forecasts), and did not interrupt the narrations except at the child's request. This method, which basically followed the child's interests, could be difficult to achieve in a class of 30 children especially when teachers' agendas are circumscribed by the demands of the National Curriculum. A classroom culture of storytelling will always be different from a home one. Stories to tell will be based on stories the teacher has told and read to the whole class, as well as other shared school experiences. Parents have a contribution to make in the classroom. Inviting them in at storytimes, or to help with reading, or to read stories to their own or other children, are ways of bringing home cultures into school and school cultures into home. In most children's homes there will be shared reading going on that teachers may not be aware of, as I found when talking to parents at a local school recently. In interviews with 19 sets of parents I found that some reading was happening at home in all cases, even though teachers had been doubtful that this would turn out to be the case. Most children had bedtime stories, and in some cases grandmothers were the key figures in providing reading experiences. Most parents did not name the sort of titles to be found in school, but they were discovering good picture storybooks from their involvement in their children's classrooms. They were also reading library books to their children, both those which came from family visits to the library and those which the child brought home from school visits to the library. Allowing parents to sit and read to children in the classroom has two-way benefits. Parents remarked to me that they were getting some idea of how other children were reading, and were able to see where their own child fitted into the reading development of the whole class. These parents were not panicking or putting extra pressure on their children, but were seeing that it was worth taking home-school reading seriously. They were also able to see the kinds of books available in the classroom, and expand their notions of what was on offer in children's literature today. Many parents of reception children reported that their four or five year old was 'reading' stories to a baby or younger sibling at home. For teachers there are also benefits. They are able to see how well parents know their own children (something which, surprisingly, can be forgotten, particularly by teachers who are not parents themselves), how parents and children relate to one another, and which stories are mutually enjoyed. Teachers who encourage parents to make written comments on their child's reading at home are learning a lot from parents. Parents are quite capable of tape-recording that child who tells stories to her baby brother and usually respond positively when invited by a teacher to contribute some data or material on their own children that the teacher might find helpful. In my own study I was saddened by the fact that the children's teachers were unaware of the storytelling that was taking place at home. My five children were not invited to tell stories in school, and two of them were perceived by their teachers to be lacking language, too quiet, and immature linguistically. Such impressions might have been overturned by hearing what the children were able to do at home. A good clear tape-recorded story, collected under the favourable conditions of one-to-one adult/child attention at home, can be played to other children (and parents who are in the classroom) and become the model for starting a storytelling culture.

The parents in my study were interested in children's books, enjoyed reading them aloud, knew quite a lot about them, borrowed them from the library, talked about books, and often bought books for their children. Consequently these parents were able to recognise the transformations from book stories that appeared in the children's invented narratives — after all they knew the stories very well themselves having read some of them dozens of times to their children. Many infant teachers regard such backgrounds as highly advantageous for the child beginning school, and, conversely, tend to regard children who do not have such rich early book experiences as disadvantaged. Yet the judgements about the nature of that so-called disadvantage can be based on little or no evidence. All the parents I spoke to at the Brighton school recently claimed to buy books for their children, and most went to the library too. Shirley Brice Heath, in her study of the working-class communities of Trackton and Roadville in *Ways With Words,* was able to show a wealth of literacy experiences going on in children's homes, which schools took very little account of. It is not likely that the majority of children have parents with an extensive knowledge of children's literature, though this is an expertise that we can expect teachers to have, and it is unhelpful to think of children as disadvantaged in this respect. There are factors which can make extensive book reading at home very problematic. I had good reason to think about these recently in South Africa, where many people are simply not in a position to give their children rich early reading experiences. In both countries there may be time factors where parents are busy working, poor housing and overcrowding, poverty, unemployment, the closure of branch libraries, the remoteness of bookshops, and even the lack of literacy of parents themselves. Valuing whatever it is that parents can and are doing, is much more positive and helpful for children than regarding them as somehow lacking if they do not come from backgrounds with extensive knowledge of children's books.

The books referred to, in the form of both transformed (disguised) material, and story retellings, by the children in my study, largely coincided with the books to be found in infant school classrooms. However, the parents I spoke to recently were not able to recall titles of favourite picture storybooks that teachers would recognise. They did tend to mention fairy tales, though — many parents mentioned *Beauty And The Beast,* a recent Disney film. In my own study fairy tales were very important, and probably provided all five children with a fundamental model of story structure and fantasy themes. All my children used the 'Once upon a time' opening for storytelling. Josh retold Hansel and Gretel eight times, and transformed parts of it in several invented stories. A whole series of very long invented stories told by Josh at about age five and a half were loosely based on *The Wizard of Oz,* though he only directly retold that story once. Another powerful story for Josh, transformed endlessly in the first 30 stories he told, was *Burglar Bill* (Allan and Janet Ahlberg). Though this is a modern picture storybook it owes everything to the structure of fairy tales, both in the language of its repeated formulae and it its powerful themes, ending in a marriage on the final page. Robert, the youngest child in the study at 3 and a half, retold *The Three Little Pigs* twice, and also used *Burglar Bill* for story retelling. Sundari transformed the story *King Midas and The Golden Touch*. Books at home and at school will probably never be alike, but what they have in common are fairy and folk tales. This will be true too for children from non-British cultures. Fairy tales are familiar to most parents — even those who do not read to their children at home — and can form the basis of a common reading culture between home and school. Fairy tales are still very much a part of modern everyday life. They are used in TV advertisements all the time — surely an acknowledgement by advertisers that they will be recognised by most people, they appear in comics, they are part of TV and film cartoons, and they are staged at Christmas in pantomimes and the like. Teachers could mount displays of different versions of fairy tales especially when new fairy tale films are on release, and perhaps try sending more than one version of a fairy tale home with the child. Parents could be encouraged to retell fairy tales themselves, and help their children to make new book versions. Such activities would help parents to feel that reading at school is familiar and friendly, taking in their own experiences as children and providing some continuity with it. For children who are not used to making up their own stories, spontaneously retelling familiar tales is a way out for both teacher and taught. By inviting children to change fairy tales, teachers can relieve them of the burden of inventing everything at once — especially the plot, which is the part of storytelling that most young children find difficult.

The children in my storytelling study did not invent bland stories. Recalling many fairy tales, the children's stories included quite a lot of violence, occasional bits of rudeness, and lots of silliness and fun. This is entirely consistent with other collections of children's invented stories (Pitcher and Prelinger 1963, Sutton-Smith 1981). Sundari tells a story about a cruel mother who confines her daughters to a corner of the house to live on crusts —

and they lived in the teeniest weeniest bit because their mother was rotten and she whipped them she said one day because they were being naughty You're horrible you children so they crept into that tiny bit... (Sundari story19)

Josh invented parodies of new broadcasts and weather forecasts. These are meant to be funny, but occasionally Josh steps into more daring, scatological territory —

it'll be sunny on the mouth of Newcastle it'll be very rainy on the nose of Newcastle (laughs) and it'll be very nice and silly on the head of Newcastle and it'll be very wet on the tinkle of Newcastle (laughs) and it will be lovely and warm in the South of the ear (laughs) and it will be very nice and smudgey and soft and warm (laughs) in the West bum... (Josh story 83)

The parents who were recording passages like these from their children were possibly prepared to be more tolerant than other parents would want to be. Children at home are on safe ground and are able to judge what their parents will laugh at and what they might dislike. In school, teachers need to think about all the children and their parents, and are also more distanced from their pupils than parents are. But children themselves have a very finely-tuned sense of what is appropriate in each place, and teacher in school will probably hear very different kinds of story. If the story telling culture of school is rich — in fairy tales for example — the stories told in the classroom will reflect this. If the stories of the classroom are dominated by the bland and dreary tales of some reading schemes, then again the children's storytelling will also reflect blandness. The sense of excitement and over-the-topness that comes through my children's stories is less a matter of story events than a matter of the language used to tell them. The five children showed an enormous interest in words, coining and inventing them in the style of Edward Lear and Lewis

Carroll, interchanging the grammatical functions of words, inventing long lists, piling up adjectives, and finding sets of synonyms. All of this happened spontaneously during storytelling, and could not have been the result of reflection. It was a matter of the children's expectation of what stories would sound like and what sort of language they would use. When Sundari makes up a nonsense story along the lines of *The Quangle-Wangle Quee* she shows that she has internalised what it is that Lear does with words to produce his strange and bizarre effects. Using his pattern of two two-syllable rhymes followed by a single syllable word using the same consonants she produces 'coggly woggly wogs' and 'piggly poggly pogs'. We know that this sort of phonological awareness is a good predictor of reading success (Bradley and Bryant 1984), and that is is learned through experience of songs, verses, rhymes and linguistically interesting oral and written texts. Some parents may well have reservations about certain types of story material. Parents who belonged to a religious group told me they sometimes worried about the number of stories with witches in them that their child was exposed to in school. Even if some kinds of story are resisted by parents, however, we need not worry as long as children are given stories which are rich in their language.

Although the children in my study, excluding Sundari, did see television in their pre-school years, TV material hardly ever appears in their invented stories. When Brian Sutton-Smith and his team collected large numbers of stories from children in American schools, including young children in kindergartens, he found that in the social setting of the classrooms children drew extensively on TV material. I believe that when children tell stories they take their audience into account. If the audience is Mum or the family they will reflect what is seen and shared as story material in the family. There were parts of all my children's stories that parents had to explain or decipher for me because I did not share the culture of that particular family. This was especially true of invented names and jokes. In school children may be quite correct in assuming that most people see and talk about TV, so they tell stories about what everyone will understand. In Sutton-Smith's study, too, he found that children would pick up story themes from other storytellers in the group, so that everybody would tell a Bugs Bunny story for example. However, there is a role for teachers in proposing and suggesting story material, particularly material that children know and can easily change. TV stories may not involve 'bookish' language in the telling, but they will involve structure, attention to the language of the telling, and linguistic and narrative skill. The parents in my study did not reject anything that was offered as a story, and while some teachers may well perceive that their pupils need stories from other sources than TV, and may focus on book stories in the interest of developing childrens reading, nevertheless TV stories should not be rejected. Children learn to do the voices (Meek, 1991), to tune in to the rhythms and structures of different kinds of language, from TV as well as from books.

What was more striking than the non-appearance of TV material in my children's stories, was the almost total absence of stories that were direct accounts of everyday autobiographical material. The children clearly preferred fantasy, and their concept of what a story is, involved fantasy. Chukovsky (1925) tells us that young children need fantasy material to sort out their concepts of what is real and will turn to more realistic material at a later age. In many schools it is common practice to have children 'share' real events that have happened in their lives at sharing time or circle time in the morning. While this activity gives children good practice in narrating or explaining to others, I have never understood why sharing time must involve real events. Perhaps some teacher fear the very length of the stories children would tell if they were allowed to make them up. But using real events does privilege those children who are already privileged in having more interesting things happen to them. The child who has most to say at sharing time is the one who was taken out or received a present or went to a party. What of those to whom such things never, or rarely, happen? And those children who may have suffered quite negative or even traumatic events at home? Fantasy can liberate us all from the restrictions of real here-and-now experience, and gives an opportunity to everybody to participate. Children can also be encouraged to talk about memories, which usually take a story form, and which need not always be about acquisitions or trips — what about being lost, being frightened, talking about baby brothers and sisters, and so on. Children could say what they would like to happen rather than be confined to what did. Fantasy sharing at circle time could be a way of starting a storytelling culture in the classroom.

The children in my study told their stories to the tape recorder, even though a parent, and sometimes other members of the family, were present during recording. Unless the children needed some help in the middle of a storytelling they tended to ignore whomever was physically present, regarding the story as an uninterrupted monologue, a performance. When they left the narrating to ask the present parent a question, they changed intonation, signalling that they were temporarily leaving the monologue. Sundari invented a first-person narrator to tell her stories, a narrator who frequently butted into the narrative to make comments, tell us about herself, and direct the events of the story. Even when her mother was present during recording it was quite clear that Sundari's narrator's interpolations were addressed to any listener to her tape, rather than to the present company. Sometimes Sundari recorded stories alone, yet her highly interactive narrator is still woven into the tale she tells. Josh used a hidden third-person narrator to tell his stories but that narrator still surfaced from time to time, asking rhetorical questions which were clearly not intended to be answered by his mother, who was sitting beside him as he spoke. To include a narrator as well as the narrated in a story makes the telling more complicated, and involves the storyteller in two kinds of narrative time, the time of the telling and the time of the told. Children who know that stories are told in this way learn to grapple with complex variations of tense and chronology, variations much more demanding than the chronological order which the National Curriculum requires older pupils to master. The very act of moving between narrating and narrated which Sundari accomplished so well would have helped her to develop an explicit understanding that stories are composed by storytellers, who imagine them and construct them from words. Until children acquire this understanding they cannot see that the characters in stories like *Come Away From The Water Shirley* (Burningham 1977) are using their imaginations to create alternative realities, just as the author of the book itself has done. This perception may seem obvious to adult readers, but inexperienced child readers often do not understand that Shirley is not really fighting with pirates and digging up buried treasure. Storytelling helps children to become explicitly aware of the activity and power of their own imaginations, showing them that stories do not arrive in books from nowhere but get made up in the author's head. Reading and talking about different versions of stories also helps to develop this understanding — an under-standing which will be a powerful aid to future reading and writing of fiction.

If the act of storytelling itself heightened the five children's awareness of constructing a world from words alone, the fact that they were tape recording themselves must have added to the metalinguistic and metanarrative gains they made. All the children always insisted on listening to the story they had just told, becoming the immediate audience for their own compositions. Often they would then go on to tell another story, which would sometimes refine or change in some way, the previous telling. In Josh's case, stories often run in series, where he attempts to work and rework the same material. For example, about half-way through his storytelling year he retells Frank L Baum's (1990) *The Wizard of Oz*. In subsequent stories he uses elements of the Baum fairytale, but transposes Dorothy and her three friends into the fictional Josh and a group of boys. The children leave home and explore mountains and valleys in much the same way that Dorothy does, usually ending in another world that resembles Baum's Oz. After a whole series of these tales, Josh finally moves into a complete transformation of the original, telling a story which is set in Heaven and which has God and St Peter as the main characters. Josh starts this story with the idea, taken from *The Wizard of Oz,* of the puppy left behind in the Emerald City, but as God and St Peter discuss ways to dispose of the puppy and finally return him to his owners on earth, they find themselves faced with a succession of other inappropriate visitors to Heaven, including Dracula, Frankenstein, and a dragon. Josh's story is very long and is a highly complex narrative, given that it is the spontaneous invention of a five-year old. In my view it is less a fluke or miracle than the result of patient and long-term reworking of a whole set of ideas and themes, most of which had their origin in stories he had heard. The advantage of using the tape recorder was that the stories were less ephemeral, more open to reordering and reworking as the children became the audience to themselves. The process of listening to oneself telling stories must in some ways be similar to the process of drafting and redrafting in writing. It is certainly a very good way to help children become aware that a first version need not be a final version, but that what we compose ourselves can be endlessly changed, adapted, and improved upon.

If using tape-recorders brought the kind of metalinguistic spin-offs I have just described, it also helped the children to understand both sides of storytelling, the teller and the audience. A distinctive characteristic of the five children's stories is the inclusion in them of a very strong sense of the listener, and internalisation of the audience to the story as part of the act of imagining necessary to do the telling. It is as though the tape-recorder acted as the page would in writing, and the children understood that what they told would be heard in some distant time and place where they themselves, the authors of the stories, could not be present to elaborate or explain any further. In learning to write, children also need to understand that their words must do all the work of communicating meaning, that the reader will read the text in the absence of the writer and the words will have to stand by themselves. The five children's narratives are often over-explicit, as though they feared leaving anything to chance; all is explained or elaborated upon, reducing thereby the risk that the listener may misunderstand the story. This is quite a conceptual leap for young children in the process of acquiring literacy. Whereas they have previously communicated in face-to-face situations where addresser and addressee are helped by the context, in writing, the context must be supplied inside the text and communicated by words alone. Telling stories into a tape-recorder, becoming your own audience for those stories, and then internalising what that audience needs, can therefore become important steps in learning to write.

Tape-recorders do not seem to be part of the resources of most Infant classrooms. The very numbers of children in classes, the noise levels generated by large groups of 5 and 6 year olds, and the lack of space to make viable recordings are often cited as reasons why tape-recorders are regarded as inappropriate at this stage.

Though these are very real problems, we need to think about what is possible. As I have suggested earlier, teachers may be surprised by the willingness of some parents to make tapes of their own children at home. Even if the teacher never found time to transcribe such tapes, it is possible that her view of certain children's spoken language competences could be reversed by merely listening to them. If spaces can be found just outside the classroom small groups or pairs of children are quite capable of making a recording without the teacher present. One or two successful recordings can fascinate other children, who can then try it themselves. Such oral stories can form the basis for writing too. Children can record the stories which they pretend- read from books, can record story retellings, and record changed versions of well-known stories. Such recordings can become part of the classroom resource base along with teachers own recordings of stories both read and invented. Even when tape-recorders are part of classroom equipment it is common to find only one machine, whereas five or six cassette players with built-in microphones would probably ensure less marginalisation of this activity. Helping to make recordings could certainly become a classroom practice for parent helpers to be involved in, which in turn could help generate more storytelling at home.

I hope these suggestions do not seem Utopian to teachers who are hard-pressed even to find sufficient book resources for their classrooms. In a technological age when computers have become standard equipment in many schools I often feel that the potential of simple cassette players has been overlooked, particularly at the stage of literacy acquisition when most children experience a gap between what they are capable of composing in words, and what they are able to write down on paper.

Although I have written extensively about the linguistic, cognitive, and affective gains, children make from story reading/

43

telling, it is important to realise, of course, that young children themselves are unlikely to look upon storytelling as anything but an enjoyable and satisfying part of their play. In encouraging storytelling at home and at school we are not really doing anything startlingly new. Role-play and story are not only a natural part of many childrens play but they are also very much alive in cultures which are not fully literate. When students and staff at the University of the Witwatersrand recorded African children telling stories during my visit in 1994, it was obvious that the recordings revealed talents and competences which had been hidden. We cannot afford to exclude children's oral language skills from our accounts of what they can do, but must really harness those skills both for their own intrinsic worth and for the literacies of the future.

References

Ahlberg J and A (1977) *Burglar Bill*. London: Heinemann.

Baum L Frank (1900) *The Wizard Of Oz*. Chicago: Rand McNally.

Burningham John (1977) *Come Away From The Water Shirley*. London: Jonathan Cape.

Bradley L and Bryant P (1984) *Children's Reading Problems*. Oxford: Basil Blackwell

Chukovsky K (1925 Trans. 1963) *From Two To Five*. Berkeley, Ca: University of California Press.

Fox C (1993) *At The Very Edge Of The Forest*. London: Cassell.

Heath Shirley Brice (1983) *Ways With Words*. Cambridge: Cambridge University Press.

Meek M (1991) *On Being Literate*. London: Bodley Head.

Pitcher E G and Prelinger E (1963) *Children Tell Stories*. New York: International Universities Press.

Sutton-Smith B (1981) *The Folk Stories Of Children*. Philadelphia: University of Pennsylvania Press.

Chapter 4

The role of the adult in supporting literacy development.

Robin Campbell

It is important that we should not underestimate the role of the adult as a support for children's literacy development. Recently Frank Smith (1992) indicated that 'Methods can never ensure that children learn to read. Children must learn from people.' That quote encapsulated, very neatly, the key role of adults. Those adults, often parents at home and teachers at school, will provide and then support children in a variety of literacy activities which serves to facilitate the children in their literacy development (Campbell, 1990).

What are some of those literacy activities — especially in the early years? And, how do the adults at home, in pre-school playgroups, in nursery classrooms and infant school classrooms use the literacy activities to support the children's learning? There are, of course, many different opportunities for children to engage with literacy. However, six particular activities will be emphasised here. They are story reading, using environmental print, momentary engagements with print, shared book experience, shared reading and opportunities for writing.

Story reading

The importance of story reading is recognised widely. For instance, the research project on children's literacy development conducted by Gordon Wells (Wells, 1986) indicated the important contribution provided by regular story readings upon children's subsequent ability with reading and writing. During such story readings children learn new words, sentence patterns and arrangements of discourse. The implicit learning of story structure helps them with their own reading and their attempts at story writing. They also learn about ways of behaving and social relationships as well as of disappointments which might be best met first in the safety of books before being encountered in real life.

Of course the story readings by the parents at home and the teachers in school require careful thought. The books to be read have to be selected with care and read skilfully. It is not a ritualised end of day activity but an important feature of the child's day. And we recognise that when young children hear a story reading they will want to participate in that reading by asking questions and making comments. The role of the adult is then to respond to such questions and comments as well as trying to get the reading back to the story line. A teacher with a reception class (Campbell, 1990) demonstrated those moves from the story to the children's queries and back to the story:

Teacher: Shall we have the story of 'Bertie at the Dentist's'?
Children: [Laughter]

Teacher:	Who do you think Bertie is?
	Sonny?
Sonny:	Hippopotamus.
Teacher:	He's a Hippopotamus.
	Do you think he's a real one?
Children:	No.
	A toy one.
Teacher:	Richard, what do you think?
Richard:	A toy one.
Teacher:	A toy one.

That brief discussion of the story, centred on the illustration of the front cover and enabled the teacher to introduce one of the main characters. Although the children recognised that the hippo was a toy one that would not hinder their subsequent acceptance of the various antics that Bertie was to get up to while Thomas, the boy in the story, was in the dentist's chair. Following that brief introduction, which the teacher might extend on other occasions, the teacher began to read the story:

Teacher:	Shall we see what happens to 'Bertie at the Dentist's'?
	Bertie was Thomas's toy hippo. They went everywhere together. On the day that Thomas had to go to the dentist's for a check up, he took Bertie along.
	There he is taking Bertie.
Michael:	Bertie can't walk.
Teacher:	No, Bertie can't walk can he?
	'Hop up here, Thomas,' said the dentist.
	'Let's take a look.'
	Thomas climbed on to the dentist's chair.
Richard:	It goes up.

Teacher: It does go up, doesn't it, Richard, yes.

Bertie sat on his tummy and watched. The chair sank back. Then it shot up into the air.

Children: [Laughter]

Teacher: Bertie nearly fell off.

Katrina: He didn't though.

Teacher: No, he didn't.

Why do you think he nearly fell off?

Katrina: Because he's on the edge of the arm.

Teacher: He nearly fell over the edge of the arm, yes.

So, the teacher provided a model of reading as the story was read and moved from the story to the children's queries and back to the story. Those responses to the children's queries would support the children's moves towards literacy. The teacher also asked 'Why?' questions so that the children would be guided towards their own construction of the story. Although, an initial perusal of such transcripts might suggest that the story-reading is somewhat disjointed, in reality such interactions flow, and they provide support for younger children to a greater extent than might a straight uninterrupted reading of the book (Dickinson and Smith, 1994).

Environmental print

Children, in our society, are surrounded by environmental print which they see adults using on a day-to-day basis. And, if in addition, the adults talk about that print with the child, or children, then the children are supported in their endeavours to understand that aspect of their world. A number of writers, frequently mothers or fathers of young children, have detailed the way in which those children learn something about print (e.g. Baghban, 1984; Laminack, 1991). Of course, we know that it can be the key features of colour, size, logo, additional pictures and context rather than the letters and words which initially enable the child to recognise environmental print. Nevertheless, children can learn about literacy if the significant adults point to and talks about the print in the environment.

In school the teacher can use that knowledge about, and interest in, environmental print to encourage children's reading and writing. In a nursery classroom, the day after the children had heard the story reading of Goldilocks and the Three Bears, the teacher prepared some porridge in the classroom for the children. Therefore, when they entered the room in the morning there was was some hot porridge bubbling in a pan (protected by an adult). Inevitably the porridge led to a great deal of excitement. But first, before the children could sample some of the porridge they were taken by the teacher for a walk — just like the three bears — so that the porridge could cool.

Once back in the classroom the children were able to try the porridge for themselves with milk or without milk, adding sugar or salt or nothing at all. For the majority of the children it was the first time that they had seen or tasted porridge, and some of the children were reluctant to try the porridge — so they had none. The teacher was aware that there might be some reluctance. So in addition to preparing the porridge she had also brought into the classroom a dozen small cereal boxes and they were used additionally to ask the children to reflect upon their knowledge of environmental print:

Teacher: Who can pick out what they had for breakfast?
Samantha: Cornflakes.
Teacher: Can you go and take the cornflakes packet?
Samantha: This one.
Teacher: How do know it is the cornflakes?
Samantha: 'Cos I do.
Teacher: Why?

Samantha:	'Cos its got a chicken.
Teacher:	Mmh, anything else.
Samantha:	The writing says cornflakes.
Teacher:	That's right.
	That says cornflakes, doesn't it.
Samantha:	And you can see the picture.
Teacher:	Yes, you can.

Of course, it was not possible to say what enabled Samantha to select the cornflakes although the pictures and the writing were mentioned. Nevertheless, like other children in the class she was able to demonstrate her use of the features on a packet in order to recognise that packet. She was aided in that learning by the teacher who provided the opportunity for the learning to occur through an interaction, with appropriate support given.

Momentary engagements with print

Denny Taylor (1983) in her various studies of young children learning to read, at home within the family, made reference to momentary engagements with print by young children. We know that toddlers will investigate their environment, move around the house looking at objects, picking up items, opening drawers and considering the contents etc. Where the adults in those homes also provide readily available books for the child then on their wanderings the child will be seen to pause, sit or lay on the floor, and look through a book before moving on to other activities. They will engage with print for a moment.

However, it is insufficient for the adult just to provide the books. The child needs to know what to do with the book and what can be expected from it. So, over the weeks and months of the child's first few years the adult will want to model the use of a book, sometimes when reading to oneself and sometimes when reading a story to a child. Those interactions between the adult and the child may involve a talk about the book as the adult turns the pages for a very young child or later, perhaps, follows the page turning of an older toddler:

Father:	Now, shall we read this book?
Robert:	(Gurgles)
Father:	Let's see what's on the first page.
Robert:	(Babbles)
Father:	Yes, it's an elephant isn't it?
Robert:	(Utters an intonation pattern which bears some resemblance to elephant).
Father:	He's a big elephant isn't he?
	And he's got big ears.
Robert:	(Coos an agreement).
Father:	Now, let's see what it's going to do.
	Oh dear.
	Just like you, he's going to have a bath.
Robert:	(Smiles).

In that instance the eleven month old was enjoying the pictures and the comments from his father. However, the interaction provided a background and foundation for Robert to know how to engage with print when he wandered about the house. In the same way if the young child at home has access to writing materials, and has seen adults using those materials, then the momentary engagement may be with writing at times and reading on other occasions.

In the school context we need to ask whether we have provided print materials, which are readily available for the children to use. Furthermore, we have to consider the extent to which we have provided models of reading and writing, and interactions with the child about literacy. All of that gives a background for the children to engage with print when their purposes lead them in that direction.

Shared book experience

Story reading is a very important part of the nursery and infant classroom day which teachers will want to continue to use. Nevertheless, as Don Holdaway (1978) noted, with a large class a number of the children may miss out on some of the aspects that might occur at home during a one-to-one story reading. At the simplest level the children may not be able to see the print and therefore fail to recognise what the teacher is doing when a story is read. Such concerns lead to his suggestion of constructing big books (now more readily available for purchase) and having a shared book experience where the teacher reads from the big book and the children can see the pictures and the writing.

An example of a shared book experience is taken from a nursery classroom with a class of four year olds:

Teacher:	Shall we have a look at this book?
Children:	Yes.
Teacher:	So what do you think it is about?
Danny:	A baby bear.
Teacher:	About a baby bear, right.
	How do you know it's going to be about a baby bear?
Danny:	'Cos it's little.
Jade:	You can see the picture.
Teacher:	That's right the picture, Jade.
	Is there anything else that tells us it might be about a teddy bear?
Georgia:	The writing.
Teacher:	Where's the writing?
Georgia:	At the top of the picture.
Teacher:	That's right at the top of the picture.
Rachel:	We could colour that in.
Teacher:	Yes, we could, couldn't we?

It says
> Teddy Bear,
> Teddy Bear.

Shall we start?

Children:	Yeah.
Teacher:	Right, what do you think the Teddy Bear is doing in this picture?
Leigh-Anne:	Playing.
Teacher:	Playing, yes. Does anyone think it is doing something else?
Russell:	It's turning around.
Teacher:	Good boy. I think Russell might be right, he says it's turning around.

Shall we read what it says?
> Teddy Bear, Teddy Bear,
> Turn around.

You were right Russell, yes.

As with the story reading in the classroom the nursery teacher reads from the big book but also engages in a dialogue with the children about the book. As part of the dialogue the children are asked to justify their comments 'How do you know...', and the teacher responded to their comments. Additionally, the writing at the top of the page was noted, and when the teacher read the captions, a pointer was used so that the children could see where the words were printed.

During such shared book experience the teacher may not be teaching reading directly, but the children were informed about the print, and the teacher modelled the reading for them. That modelling was extended in the example above, because, when the book was completed the teacher and the children read through the book once more. However, that reading took place without interruption, because the children were encouraged to read alongside the teacher or as an echo of the reading. The teacher's strategies were helping the children to learn about reading and, in part, to read.

The use of big books, or teacher-constructed big sheets/books, can also be used to model writing. For instance, when the children are reciting a nursery rhyme with the teacher he/she might ask the children for help to write that rhyme on to a big sheet. During that process the children can supply the words and the teacher can write, from the children's instructions, the nursery rhyme. So the children will see the teacher construct some writing and the teacher can talk about the writing as it is constructed. Of course, the example of using nursery rhymes is an appropriate one to utilise because we know from a number of research studies (e.g. Goswami and Bryant, 1990) that children develop a phonemic awareness, and especially an awareness of onset and rime, from engaging frequently with the sounds and rhymes of nursery rhyme favourites. That can help in their subsequent development as readers.

Shared reading

We have noted already how children will take part in story readings by making comments about the story, asking questions about it or relating the story to their own personal experiences. Furthermore, we have seen how the adult will expect the child to take part in a conversation about a book, and do so even before the child has the words necessary to make a substantial contribution to those conversations. Those events lead naturally to the one-to-one shared readings between an adult and a child which are part of home and school life. In particular shared readings are an important feature of the infant classroom. For instance five-year old Richard shared his book with his teacher:

Richard: I've got The Hungry Caterpillar.

Teacher: It is The Hungry Caterpillar, isn't it?

                    Shall we read it together?

Richard: Yeah.

Teacher: Come on then.

                    In

Richard: In the

T/R: light

Richard: of the moon

                the-the(a)

T/R   little

Richard: egg

Teacher: Yes.

Richard: lay on a leaf.

Teacher: Yes

                    It lay on a leaf, didn't it?

                    Can you see the egg?

Richard: Yeah-Yeah.

                    Yeah but the other day I looked at the picture and

                    I thought it was a hole.

Teacher: Did you? (Laughs)

                    Come on then.

R/T: One

Richard: Summer(Sunday)

                    My mum's got The Hungry Caterpillar — it's —

                    my mum's got — I've got that book like you.

                      One Summer's(Sunday) day(morning) the

                      warm sun came out(up) and — pop! — //

                  Eh.

T/R   out

Richard: of the egg

                a very(came)

Teacher:	came
Richard:	came a tiny and very hungry caterpillar.
Teacher:	It did come up didn't it, one morning.
	Yes.

Although only a small part of the interaction was presented above (the complete transcription has been presented elsewhere — Campbell, 1992) nevertheless the efforts of the teacher to support the developing reader were evident. Even the opening comment by the teacher 'Shall we read it together?' was suggestive to the five year old that he would get support from the teacher in a collaborative reading. There was no suggestion of the reading performance being tested, and, providing the teacher matched that comment with subsequent supportive comment and guidance then the child was likely to find the interaction enjoyable as well as instructive.

Of course, as we might expect, Richard did miscue some words including the(a), Summer's(Sunday), day(morning), and out(up). However, none of those miscues disrupted the meaning of the story and, therefore, the teacher did not mediate. Nevertheless, it is interesting to note how the teacher both encouraged Richard and provided a model of part of the reading by commenting 'It did come up didn't it one morning, yes.' More directly, his miscue of a very(came) did receive some teacher guidance with the text word, 'came', being provided.

Many infant teachers do organise their classrooms with great care and skill so that they can engage in one-to-one shared readings with the children. They do so because it enables them to model the reading, in some cases, and subsequently to support, guide and encourage the children's own reading of the book. Furthermore, those interactions help the teacher to ascertain the child's current progress as a reader and therefore suggest what strategies might be employed to support the child's future literacy development.

Opportunities for writing

In the earlier sections the emphasis has been on a variety of reading experiences. However, the children will also learn about print and literacy by writing. Therefore, we need to ensure that in the classroom there are opportunities for the children to write. Those opportunities can be provided in number of ways. Typically, young children have a play area/home corner in nursery and infant classrooms. Those play areas support the children's learning and growth in many ways. However, the area can also be used to encourage an involvement with literacy. Hall and Abbott (1991) indicated, with some very practical examples provided by class teachers, the way in which a play area could first be arranged to serve some particular function and second, could have materials added in order to encourage literacy. After all 'the dentist's' would need some magazines in the waiting area, posters, appointment cards, forms etc. Even more simply, a telephone message pad sited next to the telephone can be used to note messages — especially if that is modelled first by the teacher.

In one nursery classroom, where a telephone pad was added to the play area next to the telephone, the children quickly became regular writers of notes. Of course, some of those notes produced by the three year olds appeared to be no more than scribbles. However, other children included some letters, or shapes which approximated to letters, in their writing. While some children produced lines of letters — although that writing was not easily decipherable as a message.

As well as the writing opportunities in the play area, a writing centre as part of the classroom organisation adds to the opportunities for the child to write. The teacher needs to organise a table and some chairs, together with a variety of paper shapes and sizes, and writing implements. For younger children it might also be necessary to model writing occasionally and to sit with the children to talk about the writing from time to time. During such conversations the children will tell the teacher about what they have written. Those conversations can be informative, for example, when four-year old Russell, in a nursery classroom, told his teacher about his writing (which was linked to his picture of a monster):

o m l o w o

o l m m o

he indicated that it said 'One monster talking with other monsters.'; that provided insights into the extent to which he appeared to be making sense of print. Although we should not over-extend our analysis of the the connection between his statement and the writing that he produced, nevertheless, there appears to be a suggestion of Russell beginning to use his growing awareness of language sounds when writing. The provision of opportunities to write will encourage and guide children towards an exploration of print, and that is aided when the adult, from time-to-time, models the writing and then supports the children with their own efforts.

Role of the adult

Although this article has emphasised six particular literacy activities, what will have been evident within each of those activities was the important role of the adult in ensuring that the opportunities for literacy were made available and subsequently, that the children were supported during those activities. The adult role, as it permeated each of those six literacy activities, was varied. Nevertheless, it included the need to:

provide —

the books to be read were made available at both home and school, opportunities for writing were organised.

model —

during story reading, shared book experience and shared reading the reading was modelled for the children, writing was modelled in the play area and at the writing centre.

observe —

the children were observed during their encounters with literacy so that the adult could develop the opportunities for engaging with print.

interact —

the adult worked alongside the child(ren) in order to model, support and guide.

support —

the children's comments and questions received the adult's support by an acceptance of what the child could do and some guidance towards development.

guide —

the adult used comments to guide the children towards conventional literacy.

encourage —

the efforts of the child received praise and encouragement.

instruct —

the children were provided with information when it would help their understanding.

evaluate —

the adult was evaluating the literacy activities, and the literacy of the children, in order to consider what might need to be provided in the future.

As we noted in the first paragraph Frank Smith has suggested that children must learn from people. That is a view that was supported by the research of Margaret Clark (1976) when she looked at the background of thirty-two young fluent readers when starting school. A key feature of those children's background was 'an interested adult with time to devote to them when they were interested in reading' (p102). That feature, of an interested and supportive adult, or teacher, is required at home, in pre-school and nursery classrooms and the infant classroom. Those adults are required because the children learn about literacy from them.

References

Baghban, M. (1984) *Our Daughter Learns to Read and Write*. Newark, Delaware: International Reading Association.

Campbell, R. (1990) *Reading Together*. Buckingham: Open University Press.

Campbell, R. (1992) *Reading Real Books*. Buckingham: Open University Press.

Clark, M. (1976) *Young Fluent Readers*. London: Heinemann Educational.

Dickinson, D. and Smith, M. (1994) Long-term effects of pre-school teachers' book readings on low-income children's vocabulary and story comprehension. *Reading Research Quarterly*. 29. 2. pp104-122.

Goswami, U. C. and Bryant, P. (1990) *Phonological Skills and Learning to Read*. Hove: Lawrence Erlbaum Associates.

Hall, N. and Abbott, L. (Eds) (1991) *Play in the Primary Curriculum*. London: Hodder and Stoughton.

Laminack, L. (1991) *Learning with Zachary*. Richmond Hill, Ontario: Scholastic.

Smith, F. (1992) Quote. *Reading Today*. 10. 2. p34.

Taylor, D. (1983) *Family Literacy: Young Children Learning to Read and Write*. Portsmouth, New Hampshire: Heinemann Educational Books.

Wells, G. (1986) *The Meaning Makers: Children Learning Language and Using Language to Learn*. London: Hodder and Stoughton.

Chapter 5

Supporting young children with Special Educational Needs — inclusion for all?

Sheila Wolfendale and Janine Wooster

The plan for this chapter is first, to review a number of key developments, and second, to exemplify a number of these via the presentation of a focused case-study: supporting young children with special needs in the London Borough of Newham. The philosophy is that of inclusive education, which will be defined below, and the context is past and present special needs educational legislation and the Code of Practice and their bearing upon early years provision.

Tracing key developments

Recent accounts of special educational needs in the early years (Wolfendale and Wooster, 1992, Wolfendale, 1994) have sketched a number of notable innovations. These include LEA and/or social services — funded Portage programmes; other forms of parental involvement (e.g. in assessment, see Wolfendale, 1993); learning support from a variety of personnel, including welfare/special needs assistants (Balshaw, 1991). These accounts have traced the evolution of a higher profile for the early years/SEN area from the Warnock Report, through to provisions within the 1981 Education Act, and now enshrined in the 1993 Education Act and the Code of Practice. These provisions have imposed duties upon Health and Education authorities, the growth of assessment procedures, multi disciplinary co-operation.

However, none of these guaranteed automatic or speedy take-up nor resolution of outstanding problems. The (then) Department of Education and Science was chided by a Select Committee reporting on the Working of the 1981 Education Act in 1987 for not keeping statistics on early years SEN assessments and statements; the same Committee averred that the statutory assessment procedures were not working well on behalf of young children with special educational needs, and that parents were still, on the whole, inadequately informed and supported.

However, two years later, a DES Special Educational Needs Circular (No. 22/89, now superseded entirely by the 1993 Education Act and the Code of Practice) included a page devoted to 'children under five', reiterated guidelines of good practice and cited proven examples of good practice, such as Portage.

The picture, then, was mixed and equivocal with areas of least as well as most, progress and, as with the rest of the special needs area, these anomalies led to revision of the 1981 Education Act, and its replacement (though with large areas intact) by the 1993 Education Act (Part 3 devoted to special educational needs).

The centre-piece of Part 3 is The Code of Practice which constitutes a blueprint for developing good SEN practice and to which all schools, LEAs, workers 'must have due regard'. Section 5 is on 'Assessments and Statements for Under Fives', and spells out the procedures for identifying, recognising, assessing early-appearing SEN, and transition from pre-school to school. As with the rest of the Code, assessment criteria have been clarified and sharpened.

This necessarily brief review of key developments in the Early Years/SEN area sets the scene for consideration in somewhat more detail of a number of concepts which govern present and future developments in this area. Four significant concepts are identified and discussed and salient references are given, for readers to pursue the thinking and the practice.

The rights of children and equal opportunities

The United Kingdom was one of the signatories to the United National Convention on the Rights of the Child. (Newell, 1991). Progress on realising these rights in practice has been sluggish. The 1989 Children Act is clear and explicit on children's rights, whereas recent education acts have not explicitly placed them into the legislation, although the Code of Practice comes nearer to spelling out entitlement of children with special educational needs to full educational opportunities.

The rights of children with disabilities are listed in the UN Convention; an assessment of progress towards realising rights in the UK. (CRDU, 1994) identifies a number of areas where 'action is required for compliance', eg. early years education (p.158) and services for children with special educational needs (p.159).

There has been discernible movement in early years anti-racism and equal opportunities, with many early years nurseries/centres developing written policies and procedures. The CRE (1989) draws our attention to the need to: ensure that toys and equipment are neither racist nor unduly sex-stereotyped; acknowledge legitimate cultural differences in family child rearing attitudes and practice. Siraj-Blatchford (1992) offers 'five steps forward' (p.120) to bring about equitable and non-racist early years practice, and Shah (1992) presents a code of good practice, especially for the families of young children with special needs (p.77).

Archard (1993) asserts that 'the universal provision of pre-schooling is merited on egalitarian grounds' (p.167). He concludes, 'in general there is a need for 'collective uniformity', that is, for a coherent 'nesting' of agencies concerned with children and their well-being, and a clear co-ordination of the functions of family, school, health and welfare services' (p.167).

Integration/Inclusive education

Integration, or inclusive education, which is a term that is increasingly being used, is perceived to be an equal opportunities and rights issue. Hall (1992) has referred to the 'integration salad', critically, as a pot-pourri of provision characteristic of the contemporary UK scene. He regards the location/social/functional model of integration proposed in the 1978 Warnock report as 'primitive'. His view of 'inclusion' is:

> The term has a very specific meaning implying that the child should attend his/her local school or college on a full-time basis in an age-appropriate group and be supported to function as an active member of the learning community such that it matters if he or she is not present (p.12).

The conception of inclusive education means being with and caring for one another. It calls for the embracing of a new culture which accepts these tenets as integral.

The literature on integration is growing substantially, increasingly taking international perspectives (O'Hanlon, 1993, Meijer et al, 1994). The book edited by Slee (1993) is likewise international in coverage incorporating the Canadian experience of inclusive education (Ch.6).

Inclusive principles apply, of course, across the age-spectrum, and for children with special needs in the early years, includes: their access to all services; their right to early learning/early educational experiences; their right to take their place alongside their peers; their 'best interests' to be paramount.

The local case-study described in the second part of this chapter has operated an evolving inclusive education policy since 1987.

Sharing responsibility for Special Educational Needs and Inter-agency co-operation

A survey by HMI (1991) indicated growing pockets of effective interdisciplinary support, although practice was noted to be variable. 'On the ground', there are countless examples of co-operation. Some have already been referred to and are further detailed in Wolfendale and Wooster (1992) and Wolfendale (1994), also see David (1994). There is a long history of calls for greater inter-agency co-operation, of which the latest is The Code of Practice, which seeks to encourage such links by including many reminders and guidelines at each of the Stages.

As Jones and Bilton (1994) have noted, whilst the will to co-operate is there, there have been a notable number of obstacles at the institutional/structural level which challenge easy transition towards co-operation. Attempts to solve these endemic problems include realigning separate children's services into an unified early years service in a number of local areas, (Lowndes and Riley, 1994) and one proposal in Jones and Bilton for a 'children's commissioner', is under active consideration in other authorities. The Audit Commission's (1994) suggestion of a joint 'children's service plan' is likewise intended to overcome these traditional obstacles.

Co-operation includes partnership with parents/families, and the Code of Practice is explicit about partnership principles, with guidelines for practice contained in each of the Stages of identification of assessment and intervention with special needs. This emphasis mirrors the one on partnership contained in the 1989 Children Act.

Ensuring quality service for young children with special needs

The 1989 Children Act has the notion of 'quality' enshrined within it, with the specific duties upon local authorities to make provision, to inspect, to review early years provision. There is increasing acceptance of the concept of a range of performance indicators and of quality frameworks and lists of quality indices (see Elfer and Wedge, 1992).

There have been various recent attempts to identify criteria for effective SEN/Early Years services. The National Portage Association produced a code of practice (reproduced in full in Wolfendale, 1994) which enumerates twelve criteria underlying a service such as Portage. In Carpenter (1994) Peter Mittler is of the view that the 1989 Children Act, the 1993 Education Act and associated Code of Practice, provide an opportunity for children's services to rethink the aims and objectives of early intervention and he poses a list of five questions to facilitate this exercise (p.69). In the same proceedings (Carpenter, 1994), Philippa Russell lists 'factors in developing early identification and intervention programmes' (p.39-40) which not only constitutes an agenda but a blueprint for applying quality criteria.

Post-Warnock developments in early years/SEN have been manifestly significant; young children with disabilities and special needs are less marginalised than hitherto, by virtue of expanded services (and see the next section as one exemplar), an increased knowledge-base on assessment and intervention; improved and improving staff expertise; a discernible move towards greater inter-agency co-operation and partnership with parents.

The Description of Work in Newham which now follows, provides a first-hand depiction of a number of these developments and issues.

A description of recent work with young children with Special Educational Needs based in the London Borough of Newham

To illustrate with practical examples, points made in the first half of this chapter, we will show briefly how the 'Inclusive Education' policy came to the borough and how this is operating in practice. It will be illustrated by two case studies of young children who have recently been placed in school.

When a decision was taken by the local education committee in 1986 to put in place a policy of integration, the immediate reaction of many professionals working in the area was panic. Staff working in special provisions were sure that they would lose their jobs in a very short time. Staff in mainstream schools were convinced that they would be flooded with hundreds of children who were needing very special provision during the next term and that they would not be able to cope. 'We have not been trained for this' was a cry heard throughout the borough. Of course things did not move ahead as quickly as every one thought; a gradual process of placing children in their local community schools with appropriate support was begun, alongside the very gradual process of closure and re-allocation of specialist provision. A few years later the policy changed from one of 'integration' to one of 'inclusive education', a more appropriate way of describing the phenomenon. However this change of title seemed to throw up many of the old fears and it seemed to many support staff that it was necessary to go over much of the old reassuring, and reiterate to people that there were not going to be dramatic overnight changes and that there were many examples of good practice already taking place. One method used to do this was to develop links with other places and LEAs who were also trying to implement a similar policy. For example, close links were developed with a province in Canada, with exchange visits being arranged.

Many training courses were offered, using trainers from in and out of the borough. Staff were able to gain units towards a validated DPSE by working on courses looking at 'Special needs in the ordinary school', 'Developing children's language', and 'Severe learning difficulties in the mainstream school'. Courses were offered to look at issues relating to the behaviour of pupils, and governor training schemes were set up. NNEB's and Classroom assistants were also offered training as time went on and meetings and discussions were set up in order that people could update their knowledge and discuss things that were going well, as well as things that were proving difficult. The advent of the 'Code of Practice' has meant many more opportunities for training.

It was felt that a lot depended on the first experience that schools and families had of inclusion and the need for carefully organised systems of support was clearly seen. Links were developed with other agencies, not least a close link between the local Child Development centre, and the Preschool support team and the educational psychologists. It was clearly necessary to develop close links with agencies such as community physiotherapy, occupational therapy and speech therapy, as a change in their working practice would be essential if the policy was to work in practice.

Several Inclusive initiatives have been developed in schools, offering some enhanced staffing to help those children who need very specialised care. Most recently two fully inclusive schools have been built at opposite ends of the borough, which are fully accessible and well resourced.

The learning support team has developed slowly from a number of professionals working in isolation with different ages and groups of children to a large well-resourced team, covering children from preschool, primary and secondary phases. Many of the children are referred to the team at a very young age and the Preschool team currently has a roll of almost two hundred pupils with a whole range of difficulties, from those children whose difficulties are likely to be ongoing, to those who given early support will be placed in school with minimum or no support. Of 48 children who went into school during 1993 only eight went to specialist schools or units the remainder being placed in mainstream provision with varying levels of support. The preschool element of the Learning Support team, now consists of teachers and nursery nurses who work together to try and develop the most effective and consistent way of delivering support to families and establishments who cater for preschool children. A large part of the role is to work within the systems developed under the 1981 Education Act and more recently the 1993 Education Act and the Code of Practice for the assessment of young people who may have special educational needs.

The aims and objectives of the Preschool team are as follows:

Aim

The aim of the team is to enable children with special educational needs to enter the least restrictive educational environment. This aim is in line with the borough's equal opportunities and inclusive education policies. It is set in accordance with the principles of the Children Act 1989.

Objectives

1. To raise parental awareness of the implications of their children with special educational needs entering mainstream or special nurseries and schools.

2. To provide practical support for parents of young children with special educational needs.

3. To help develop a network of parental support.

These objectives will be promoted by:

- ☐ sharing skills with parents, making suggestions for useful play activities and equipment, sometimes loaning equipment belonging to the service;

- ☐ helping to organise parent support groups, social activities and outings;

- ☐ encouraging and helping parents to attend meetings and reviews;

- ☐ offering support and guidance to parents or referring them to other support or counselling agencies for more specialised help;

- ☐ interactive work with families of children on our case load, encouraging for example the involvement of siblings;

- ☐ interactive work with children;

- ☐ accepting that other team members may have a different method of working;

☐ accepting that different learning styles exist and therefore demands made on children/adults may be different.

4. To prepare children with special educational needs for entry into educational settings and for subsequent entry into the National Curriculum, and SATs.

5. To raise awareness in mainstream nurseries, children's centres and playgroups of the implications of accommodating children with special educational needs and of their right of access to the National Curriculum.

6. To provide support for young children with special educational needs in nurseries or playgroups;

These objectives will be promoted by:

☐ working alongside other professionals in these settings to assess jointly the needs of individual children and modify practices to accommodate them;

☐ providing qualified staff to carry out the support, as agreed in consultation with the staff within these settings.

☐ providing in-service training for early years staff.

7. To develop practice in relation to young children with special educational needs.

8. To promote the interests of young children with special educational needs.

These objectives will be promoted by:

☐ in-service training within the team;

☐ provision of in-service training for other agencies;

☐ keeping accurate records for children within the caseload;

☐ producing reports and submitting educational advice to the authority on children being formally assessed;

☐ working as part of a multi-disciplinary team including parents, educational psychologists, doctors, speech therapists, occupational therapists, physiotherapists, social workers, health visitors, early years personnel in education and social service settings;

☐ evaluation and regular review of ways of working together to ensure efficient service delivery.

☐ attending and contributing to regular meetings or review at the Child Development Centre, therefore sharing information via a central record system.

9. In order to maintain high professional standards in the course of our work, it is important that all team members appreciate the value of supporting each other and offering regular opportunities to review practices.

The roles undertaken as a team are many and varied and include:

Home Visits
We see many of the children and families we support in their own homes.

We visit regularly, usually on a weekly basis, but sometimes more or less often as appropriate.

Home visits include teaching time, parental support, planning and time to discuss the child's future placement, etc.

Visits to Nursery Schools/Classes, Playgroups, Children's Centres and Primary Schools
We work with groups, nurseries and schools in order to support children with special educational needs. We try as far as possible to come to an agreement with parents and early years staff about the level and nature of this support.

We work in a variety of ways, for example we may offer structured individual support, group activities helping children to acquire social skills, language, etc, or we may take larger groups enabling staff to spend extra time with identified children.

We liaise with staff and discuss together possible difficulties and strategies for dealing with these. We also liaise over preparation of educational advice for children who are in the process of being formally assessed.

Administration Time

Administration tasks include record keeping and report writing, arranging visits or meetings, child protection work, liaising with other professionals, etc. As regular visitors to family homes we have an important role in keeping our colleagues from educational, health and social services informed of developments, and in passing on messages to others from parents. We often need to seek advice and help from other professionals.

Groups

We run two opportunity groups for children and their carers; one is held at our centre and the other at one of the inclusive provisions.

The Centre group is primarily for the families of children who have difficulties with communication. The School group caters primarily for the families of children who have multiple needs.

We are also involved with a third group run at the Child Development Centre.

Meetings

As a team we meet approximately once a week to discuss organisation and team development, and to share information.

These weekly meetings are also used for supervision and training.

Individual members of the team meet with various professionals involved with the children on their case loads, including physiotherapists, speech therapists, occupational therapists, health visitors, educational psychologists and social workers as well as other early years staff.

Informal meetings are often a great source of support and information.

Training

We organise training sessions for the whole team, sometimes inviting speakers, sometimes drawing on the expertise within the team.

We try to participate in as many courses organised by outside bodies as possible to keep up to date with developments in special needs and the early years.

We offer extensive training to early years establishments on all aspects of special needs and we contribute to the borough's early years programme of courses and input to courses for school governors.

The following two examples will illustrate how policy and practice come together when the team work with families who have a young child with special educational needs.

Mohammed — He arrived from India when he was five years old; his father is reported to be in prison back at home and Mum is alone with Mohammed. The family has no legal status and therefore is not entitled to any benefits. Due to this lack of status and a general fear of professionals Mum is unwilling to admit anyone to the home. Mohammed speaks little in English or Punjabi and Mum speaks only Punjabi. Mohammed arrives in a reception class at his local school; he is very frightened — this comes over mainly in very difficult behaviour, running around the room, climbing, hitting out, screaming, biting and scratching other children and destroying their work. He finds it very difficult to settle to a task and is constantly watching to see if anyone is going to open the door so that he can run out. After a few days he is referred to the Preschool team, links are made via an interpreter (one of the school staff) to his Mum and it appears that he is exhibiting similar, though not so severe, behaviour at home. He begins to settle down at school although any slight change in routine upsets him a great deal. As he settles down it becomes clear that he has learning difficulties in addition to the behaviour difficulties he has already exhibited. He always seems to be in the wrong and other children are always sure that it was Mohammed if anyone is crying, anything goes missing or anything is ripped or broken. At the end of the term he is seen by the Educational Psychologists and a formal assessment is begun. A programme is put in place written by the Class teacher, the learning support teacher and the educational psychologist. A new reception class is opened at the start of the new term and he is moved to a smaller group.

He will continue to receive support from a nursery nurse and from a teacher, subject to review, when it is hoped support can be gradually withdrawn, whilst ensuring the school is able to continue providing, monitoring and evaluating individual educational programmes.

Fowsia — This little girl is the third child of an Urdu-speaking family. She was born with multiple difficulties and was referred to the Preschool team shortly after leaving the Special Care Baby Unit. It soon became clear that her difficulties would be severe and continuing. She was having numerous convulsions; she was very small for her age; it was extremely difficult to feed her; her fluid intake was very small — it has been estimated that at age four years her intake of fluid was less than a six-month-old baby. Her clothes at age four were labelled twelve to eighteen months. She had regular input from the speech therapist, physio and occupational therapists and went regularly to the local hospital and Great Ormond Street as well as to the local Child

Development Centre. The family was seen regularly at home and support was provided for visits, as well as ideas for encouraging her development. She joined the group which has children with multiple needs and her family made links with other families who had children with similar kinds of difficulties. At age three and a half she was assessed and received a statement. Her parents had asked for a place in an inclusive provision, which she now attends full time. The family continues to receive some home support from the preschool team.

It is to be hoped that the support of young children with special needs will be further facilitated by the Code of Practice, operational from September 1994, with its emphasis on inclusion, rights and entitlement.

References

Archard, D. (1993) *Children, rights and childhood,* London: Routledge.

Audit Commission (1994) *Seen but not heard — co-ordinating Community Child Health and Social Services for Children in Need,* London: HMSO.

Balshaw, M. (1991) *Help in the Classroom,* London: David Fulton.

Carpenter, B. (Ed.) (1994) *Early Intervention — where are we now?* proceedings of a Conference held in Oxford, March 1994, from Westminster College, Oxford, OX2 9AT.

Code of Practice (1994) London, Department for Education/HMSO.

Commission for Racial Equality (1989) *From Cradle to School, a practical guide to race equality and childcare,* Elliott House, 10-12 Allington Street, London, SW1E 5EH.

Children's Rights Development Unit (1994) *UK Agenda for Children* 235 Shaftesbury Avenue, London WC2H 8EL.

David, T. (Ed.) (1994) *Working together for Young Children, multi-professionals in action,* London: Routledge.

Elfer, P. and Wedge, D. (1992) *Defining, measuring and supporting quality,* Ch.3 in Pugh, G. (Ed.) Contemporary issues in the early years, London: Paul Chapman and National Children's Bureau.

Hall, J. (1992) 'Token' integration: how else can we explain such odd practices? *Learning Together,* Issue 3, October, pp.9- 13.

HMI Report (1991) *Interdisciplinary Support for young Children with Special Needs,* ref. 17/91/NS, London: DFE.

Jones, A. and Bilton, K. (1994) *The Future Shape of Children's Services,* London: National Children's Bureau.

Lowndes, V. and Riley, K. (1994) Co-ordinating Services for Young Children, the implication for Management, Local Government Managing Board, Arndale House, Arndale Centre, Luton, LU1 2TS.

Meijer, C., Pijl, S., Hegarty, S. (Ed.) (1994) *New Perspectives in Special Education, a six-country study of integration,* London: Routledge.

Newell, P. (1991) *The UN Convention and Children's Rights in the UK,* London: National Children's Bureau.

O'Hanlon, C. (1993) *Special Education Integration in Europe,* London: David Fulton.

Select Committee (1987) *Special Educational Needs: implementation of the 1981 Education Act,* 3rd Report from the Education, Science and Arts Committee, Vols. 1 & 2, London: HMSO.

Shah, R. (1992) *The Silent minority, children with disabilities in Asian Families,* London: National Children's Bureau.

Siraj-Blatchford, I. (1992) *Why understanding cultural differences is not enough,* Ch.6 in Pugh, G. (Ed.) Contemporary issues in the early years, London: Paul Chapman and National Children's Bureau.

Slee, R. (Ed.) (1993) *Is there a desk with my name on it? The Politics of Integration,* London: Falmer Press.

Wolfendale, S. and Wooster, J. (1992) *Meeting Special Needs in the Early Years,* Ch.7 of Pugh, G. (Ed.) Contemporary Issues in the Early Years, London: Paul Chapman and National Children's Bureau.

Wolfendale, S. (Ed.) (1993) *Assessing Special Educational Needs,* London: Cassell.

Wolfendale, S. (1994) *Policy and Provision for children with Special Educational Needs in the Early Years,* in Riddell, S. and Brown, S. (Eds.), SEN policy in the 1990's: Warnock in the Market Place, London: Routledge.

Index

Author Index